School Days

memories of Sandwich Secondary School
1935-2010 collected by

Susan Hibberd

2nd Editiom
©Susan Hibberd 2017

This book is sold subject to the condition that it shall not, by way of trade or otherwise, be lent, resold, hired out, or otherwise circulated without the publisher's prior consent in any form of binding or cover other than that in which it is published and without a similar condition including this condition being imposed on the subsequent publisher.

British Library Cataloguing In Publication Data
A Record of this Publication is available from The British Library

The moral right of Susan Hibberd has been asserted.

ISBN 978-0-9566656-9-0

First published in Great Britain in September 2010
by Butterfly Cottage Publishing
170 Rectory Road
Deal, Kent, CT14 9NR

Also by this author:

*The Purple Butterfly -
diary of a thyroid cancer patient*

The Little Book of Collectable British Pyrex

The Butterfly Book of Kentish Recipes

The Butterfly Book of Essex Recipes

The Black Cat Gallery

The Village of Shalmsford, Kent

ABOUT THE AUTHOR

Susan Hibberd studied at the Dorset Institute of Higher Education before being awarded a BA at Southampton University. After almost a decade as an Internal Auditor in the Civil Service, and just under twenty years as the OLC Manager at Sandwich Technology School, she now devotes her time to researching and writing books.

Contents

INTRODUCTION 11
A BRIEF HISTORY OF THE SCHOOL 13
UNIFORM 29
INSPIRATIONAL STAFF 40
LESSONS 61
SCHOOL DINNERS 78
PREFECTS AND MONITORS 85
SCHOOL ASSEMBLIES 92
CLUBS AND ACTIVITIES 95
TRIPS 106
FUNDRAISING 112
THE SCHOOL PRODUCTION 114
APPENDIX 1 119

Acknowledgements

My thanks go to teachers past and present who have helped me to piece together a historical timeline charting the development of the school, and to Mrs Gomez, the current Headteacher, for allowing me access to the school archives.

Every effort has been made to contact all copyright holders. I would be pleased to hear if any omissions have occurred.

I am particularly indebted to the following people, who so generously shared their memories and photographs with me.

Name	Date left school
Andrew Frost	1958
Anthea Croucher nee Tittensor	1955
Barbara Pope nee Cook	1945
Ben Nuttall	2006
Bernard Rogers	1957
Bernard Watson	1971
Brad Head	1995
Brenda Coleman nee Elgar	1962
Brian White	1954
Brian Wilmshurst	1954
Carol Allen nee French	1976
Carol Coleman	1972
Chris Cooper	1963
David Deveson	1943
David Parfitt	1950
David Stone	1959
Dennis Parsons	1944
Doreen Anderson nee Cook	1952
Douglas Tutton	1959
Eirwen Fletcher nee Richards	1939
Francis Butler	1956
Freda Francis	1971

Glynn Tucker	1959
Grace Wray nee Ashington	1937
Helen Martin nee Croucher	1955
Ivan Beer	1950
Janet Sayer nee French	1981
John Durban	1961
Joyce Parfitt nee Bartlett	1946
Julie Rogers	1976
Kevin Summers	1977
Linda Ridden nee Saint	1972
Lisa Powell	1986
Margaret Wilmshurst	1958
Marion Humphreys nee Scott	1983
Mark Jarrett	2001
Martin Jarrett	1963
Mary Rowan nee Douglass	1974
Maureen Cullen nee Sutton	1945
Maureen Peattie nee Shelvey	1951
Michael Cowell	1959
Myra Bullows nee Gordon	1965
Myrna Cartson nee Petley	1955
Patricia (Paddy) King nee Harvey	1950
Patrick Gleeson	1959
Paul Isemonger	1971
Paul Southgate	1975
Philip Rowcroft	2006
Redmond McKinnon	1978
Rodney Betts	1957
Ron Brown	1957
Sharon Crowley nee Amos	1974
Sharon Russell nee Treadway	1978
Shirley Taylor	1977
Simon Harris	2006
Stella Leitner nee Scott	1990
Stephen Smith	1999
Stuart Watson	1955
Sylvia Roy nee Moseley	1963
Terry Sharp	1974

Valerie Dodd	1949
Valerie Hopper nee Wisdom	1949

The bike shed at the back of the school in the 1980s

Introduction

Sandwich Central School in 1938

"I remember my first day really well, September 2001. I remember walking up to the bus stop and not letting my mum walk up with me. Getting on the bus and sitting right at the front with all the other Year 7s and being the only ones there all chatting to each other and the driver. When we got to school I met up with all the people I went to primary school with. It was all so exciting and everything was new. I looked ridiculous when I look back on it with my rucksack, laptop bag and P.E. Kit. We were all herded down into the school hall and told what forms we were in. It was great - I was in a form with some of my best friends from primary! That's all I can remember of that day, just the sheer joy and excitement of finally going to 'big school'."

Ben Nuttall
writing about his first day at Sandwich Technology School in 2006.

It is not hard to believe that almost every child who attended this school had similar feelings on their first day.

However, they overcame this trepidation and all the people I interviewed have come forward with positive memories of their time here.

This book is not intended as a definitive history of the school, charting its rise from a Central School of less than 400 pupils to an Academy catering for almost 1,400, but as a record of the people who have passed through its doors.

I hope that past pupils will find pleasure in remembering teachers, lessons and out-of-school activities, and that those still at the school will take a moment to consider how far we have come. These are the people who drove the school forward and helped us to build the reputation we enjoy today.

Susan

Students on the playing field in 1956

A Brief History of the School

The school in 1935 before the double row of pink cherry trees was planted along the front.

Sandwich Central School was built on Dover Road, Sandwich during 1935 and opened its doors in May of that year. 380 students, born between 1921 and 1923 were enrolled under Mr Cook, and were divided into ten classes to be taught by twelve members of staff. Before the school opened children would have stayed at their village school until they reached the school leaving age of 14.

Such was the popularity of the school that by September of that year, the roll had increased to 468 (see appendix).

The motto that was chosen was 'Grit and Determination' and the school colours were maroon and gold. The students were divided into three houses: red, yellow and green, and students were awarded stars for attendance, progress and behaviour.

Students came to the school on foot, by bike and by bus from Sandwich and the surrounding villages, the furthest coming from Stonar in the north, Ash in the east and Ringwould in the south.

Mr Cook in later years

Just four years later, because of the war, the students returned to their village primary schools to be taught. David Parfitt remembers going back to Northborne Primary School with several others from Sandwich, while Barbara Pope and her friends went back to Eastry School.

The older children continued to come to Sandwich Central School, but were only allowed in the building sixty at a time. Therefore, students from Eastry attended in the morning, and those from Sandwich came in the afternoon.

War broke out in the summer holiday of 1939 so we never returned to school. Mr Hyde, our English teacher used to come over to Betteshanger several days a week until the school was evacuated to Wales when there was fear of German invasion.

Eirwen Fletcher

In May of 1940, 120 children were evacuated to Wales with 11 staff. The school furniture was removed and the male staff were called up for active duty. However, the school accepted children on a voluntary basis from November of that year, although they were only allowed in for an hour at a time, in groups of ten or less. On the first day 172 pupils turned up.

Some students revelled in the time they had off. Pupils like Dennis Parsons, who attended from 1941-44 loved counting the enemy fighters as they flew overhead. He remembers seeing a German pilot bail out into Caspell's Field near Eastry, and seeing the aircraft leave from Manston on their mission to sink The Bismark.

Talking of fighter planes, a great status symbol among the boys was a "bit of German aircraft" - the bigger the better. There was a lot of debris about at that time. I remember one lad coming in with an altimeter with a swastika on it. He was top dog for some time!

Andrew Frost

The school was taken over by the military in 1941, but they used the hall and practical rooms only. The rest of the school remained open for voluntary attendance until 1942, when it reopened fully.

I lived opposite the old Sandwich Central School for many years. I can well remember it being an army camp during the war, with a Polish airman parachuting into the ground during the battle of Britain.

David Deveson

Towards the end of the war, twenty children from London were evacuated *to* Sandwich and one such child was Maureen Sutton. Writing in 1986, she remembers:

I hated school before that, but I was quickly made welcome. We used to go to school every day in one of the miners' buses. I remember clearly the Cottage Homes at Eastry - picking up the children all looking the same – clothes I mean.

In 1944, the Education Act brought in selective education, and the school became Sandwich County Modern School, taking pupils who did not pass the '11-Plus' grammar school entrance exam. Students could stay on until they were 16 and take the School Certificate examination if they wished.

When the war in Europe ended in 1945, the students were granted two days holiday and those teachers who had been in the services (such as Mr Rosseter and Mr Hopper) and those students who had been evacuated began to return.

Boys outside the air-raid shelter in 1947

Students from the 1950s remember the uneven surface of the school playing field. Today, there is still a hillock, known affectionately as 'monkey hill', near the tree line.

In the war there was a deep ditch dug across the sports field, and the excavated soil left as a bank, to stop German planes or gliders landing. In my day it had been filled in, but not that well, there was still a dip and ridge showing.

Andrew Frost

In 1947, the school leaving age was raised to 15, and by the end of the year, the school catered for 566 children. To accommodate the extra pupils the government funded temporary buildings with concrete floors/walls, metal windows and corrugated asbestos roofs. The scheme was called the Hutting Operation for the Raising of the School-leaving Age and the buildings became known as 'HORSA huts'.

The HORSA huts in 1980

Life at the school returned to normal, with only a few notable incidents:

In the 1950s the US Air Force were stationed at Manston. They had large, heavy bombers and an array of fighters. All of them were noisy. They continually flew over the school. One fighter/bomber was the Thunderjet and it certainly lived up to its name. One day in about 1953 two Thunderjets collided over the school and the wreckage fell to earth in Worth.

Rodney Betts

Francis Butler remembers this incident, too:

One incident I remember was when an American Jet Fighter aircraft had engine failure and narrowly missed the school, 'belly'-landing in the field just the other side of the Deal Road. One or two of us went over to look at it at lunchtime. A couple of days later it was removed on a transporter - the wings having been removed first.

Francis Butler

Students also remember the Coronation:

My second year (1953) was the Queen's coronation when we received a coronation mug.

Bernard Rogers

The front entrance of the school in 1953

By 1954 the school motto had changed to 'Hold fast to that which is right', taken from 1 Thessalonians, but the school badge remained the same.

Each year was divided into four classes. First year was A1, A2 etc, second year was B1, B2 etc. If your 15th birthday was after September you would go to either E1 or E2.

Brian Wilmshurst

Buses waiting to take pupils home in 1954

By 1955 the school had grown, and the houses were renamed:

The school was divided into 5 houses, they being Sandwich, Ash, Wingham, Eastry and Stonar. One lad in our class was so keen that he made metal lapel badges for those that wanted one - his name was John Line.

Stewart Watson

In my day, houses were geographical: membership was based on where we came from. Eastry, Sandwich, Ash, Wingham. I can see that the new system allows membership numbers to be balanced more easily, but you must lose the territorial loyalties that made house rivalries such fun.
     Andrew Frost

School life was routine for the rest of the decade, although a few highlights broke the monotony:

In about 1956 the Queen Mother was driven from Sandwich to Deal and the school lined the playing field fence on the Deal road.

Rodney Betts

The Queen Mother came past the school one day, along the road at the bottom of the field. We all waited, spread out along the fence. The cars were going quite fast. The chauffeurs slammed on the breaks when they saw us, but by that time they were half way along the fence, so those of us who had elected to go as far away from the school as possible, down to the right hand end, only caught a glimpse of the QM.

Thinking of that road, at the time we thought that it was busy. I remember Mr. Cook giving us lectures in assembly on road safety. "I watched you cyclists this morning, you half filled the road! Please, no more than THREE abreast!" Imagine riding three abreast now.

Andrew Frost

The main part of the school beforethe new building works in 1957

Partially completed building work (1957)

CSE exams were introduced in 1965 to compliment the GCE exams that had been taught since 1951. (Both these exams were replaced by the GCSE in 1988), and a new fifth form of 30 pupils was established for those pupils who wished to take these.

One other notable event was the heavy snowfall in the early months of 1970, when 34 children and 3 staff were trapped in the school.

During the winter of '69/'70 we had a large snowstorm. Those of us who lived beyond Eastry towards Tilmanstone, Eythorne and other places in The Downs used to have to wait in the old Girls Playground for Hampshire's coach. On that day the bus never came back and we were stuck at school. We had to sleep on gym mats in the old A1 class next to the Head's office. The marines from Deal brought out blankets on a lorry.

During the night Mr Gilbert came in from his office and chatted to us. He had his shirt off and we were all shocked by the scars he had from the war- something he had kept quiet about.

Next day the school was closed but we were given a huge breakfast and lunch. After lunch the Council had cleared the road as far as Eastry and we were taken there by a Sandwich-based coach company. Then we transferred to a tractor and trailer for the next four miles to the High and Dry pub at Waldershare after which those of us from Eythorne walked the last mile and a half through four-foot plus drifts.

Bernard Watson

Freda Francis, Head Girl at the time, also remembers that night:

We had to stay at the school overnight one year because the coaches which were coming to collect us were stuck in snow. The girls were bedded out with neighbours in the road opposite. My brother Roger recalls that boys all bedded down in Room 1, next to the Headmaster's Office. There was no electricity, and when a commotion ensued because one of the lads had let a hamster loose Mr Gilbert arrived, trouser-less (so he didn't spoil his creases) carrying a candle and with a blanket draped around him to see what the noise was about! They had their evening meal in the Domestic Science room and played all evening in the gym.

Freda Francis

In 1972 the school leaving age was raised again, and pupils were required to stay at school until the year they were 16, being allowed to leave in the April of that year. However, they did get a day off for the Queen's Silver Wedding Anniversary in 1973.

Traditions were maintained at the school throughout the 1980s, including that of separating male and female pupils although the houses were renamed as Barbican, Sandown, Fishergate, and Newgate.

I attended Sandwich Secondary School from 1985 – 1990. When I first came, boys and girls were separated throughout the school with areas that were off limits to the opposite sex. The stairs in the old building were designated boys or girls and one would not dare use the wrong stairs. The playgrounds were also separate - one on the Dover Road, which was for girls, and one on the Deal Road side in the car park area, which was for boys.

Stella Leitner

Mr Elliot was appointed Headmaster in 1982 and began an era of rapid change. He spent his first year at the school immersing himself its culture and way of life. After this, he began his programme of improvements.

He abolished the practice of dividing the sexes, brought together a PTA and started a sixth form, who studied GNVQ subjects.

During the next fifteen years, the school intake increased dramatically particularly as it merged with Aylesham Secondary School in the mid 1990s.

A series of building works doubled the size of the school, and it gained a second story above the gym, a science block, a school hall, a suite of music/drama rooms, and The Elliot Wing, which runs along the front of the school.

The Elliot Wing gave the school a new front entrance.

Mr Elliot also became a trustee with the Sandwich Sports and Leisure Centre committee and negotiated the erection of the Sports Centre, which allows student access during the day. Joined to the back of the school hall, the changing rooms double as Green Rooms for the stage.

In 1991 the Queen Mother opened the centre.

I remember the Queen Mother opening the Sports Centre and landing on the field in a helicopter

Brad Head

After a brief spell as a Grant Maintained School, Technology School status was granted, and the name changed once more, to become Sandwich Technology School.

Mr Wallis was appointed as Head teacher in 1997 and continued the programme of expansion, developing a Creative Arts wing (below), which was opened in 2003 by Boy George.

When the 2003 building works were completed the school entrance was moved to the Deal Road side of the campus, and buses now deliver and pick-up students from this side only. What was the school office is now a fully equipped hair salon.

Building work continued and The Richard Wallis Centre of Excellence, was completed in 2006, which includes a restaurant, a new library and a cinema. The cinema was opened in 2005 by actress Brenda Blethyn, who later played a cameo role in a film made by the students.

The Open Learning Centre replaced the Flexible Learning Centre when the new building was opened in 2006.

Dame Kelly Holmes (seen here with sixth form student Tim Harris) presented Mr Wallis with his 'Headmaster of the Year' National Teaching Award in 2006.

The school is at the forefront of the move towards greater sustainability and is one of only 1,000 in the country to have been awarded an Eco Schools Green Flag. This 5kW wind turbine was erected in 2007.

The houses were changed again in the early 2000s to Austen, Brunel, Redgrave, Newton, Sharman, Elgar, Marlowe, and Turner but the school is now divided into just four 'colleges': Union, Liberty, Discovery and Endeavour.

Mrs Gomez was appointed as the school's first female head teacher in 2009, and took up her headship in January 2010.

The school continues to grow both physically and in its ethos. In 2009, an all-weather pitch was added to the playing field, to coincide with the opening of a Football Academy and by the end of 2010 the school hopes to have been granted Academy status.

A new logo and a new uniform will be used form September 2010 to mark the beginning of this new era.

SANDWICH
TECHNOLOGY
SCHOOL

Uniform

1930s

The uniform for the girls was maroon blazers and gymslips and cream blouses with a tie in maroon, cream and green. These were also the colours for the badge, which was a bulldog with the motto 'Grit and Determination'. For the boys it was the same, but with grey trousers. It was not possible for all pupils to have the uniform, but there was always some sort of dress code, and absolutely no jewellery of any kind.

Grace Wray

Part of a whole school photo from 1937. Note the lower school boys in long socks and shorts.

Girls wore a wine coloured pinafore with a cream shirt underneath in 1937. The PE knickers were the same maroon colour.

I remember the summer uniform. The dresses were cotton, red and white check. Year one had one button just below the front of the collar. Year two had two buttons and year three had three buttons. If I remember correctly year four had a red bow .in the same position as the buttons.

I can't quite picture the winter hat but we were always expected to wear it. When we went back after the Whitsun break we had cream panamas with a band and the school badge on the front. We looked very smart in our red and white check dresses, maroon blazers and panamas. We always wore those when we took part in the singing festivals at the Winter Garden in Margate.

If we tilted our hats so much as an inch out of line Miss Brann would have you up before her. We weren't there to make a fashion statement! Young ladies were expected to have some sense of decorum!

We didn't have skirts- our winter uniform was a dark grey gym slip, white blouses, school tie and a maroon cardigan. We wore our blazers when we returned in September. I can't recall what topcoats we wore in the winter.

Eirwen Fletcher

The school badge with the bulldog logo was sewn onto the school caps and blazers. Gold braid edge, gold braid bulldog, maroon shield

The boys had wine-red blazers, school caps, grey shorts and socks and black shoes. The blazer badge was a fierce golden bull-dog.

Mr Rosseter reminiscing in 1985

1940s

During my time, the girls wore maroon cardis.

Maureen Peattie

Mr Pagett and the School Shield Team 1945-6

1950s

Girls had maroon satin knickers to wear in PE.

Brenda Elgar

In the winter, pupils wore grey skirts or trousers. The girls had grey cardigans and short, white socks.

During the 1950s, girls were allowed to wear blue and white gingham dresses in the summer. The lower years had gingham shirt-waisters and the older girls had a dogtooth blue & white check fabric which they were allowed to have made up into whichever style they preferred.

Editor

The school badge was a originally a gold bulldog on a maroon background, but it was redesigned while I was there by Mr Burnand as a yellow dog on a grey background.

Margaret Wilmshurst

Photograph of class D1 in 1954. These students were in the top set of the year currently known as Year 10.

1960s

I remember my first day. I was waiting outside Mr Gilbert's office. My parents didn't realize that uniform was to be worn so I had arrived wearing an ordinary summer dress so I stuck out like a sore thumb.

Myra Bullows

Girls in the 1960s wore pleated, grey skirts in the winter and a blue and white striped dress in the summer.
The school blazer was still made of a thick woollen fabric.

This picture of Class A2 from 1960 shows the boys with their short trousers. Their teacher is a young Mrs Firminger.

Girls in 1964

This girls team shows the grey sports skirt. Each girl has the Kent School Athletic Association Badge sewn onto her skirt.

1970s

The uniform was blue and white throughout my time at the school.

Shirley Taylor

Maxis and minis were both 'in' in the 1970s. When everybody else was wearing mini skirts, I thought I was safe in a maxi. No such luck! I still got into trouble!

However, I still got to be a prefect and became Eastry House girls sports captain. I gained all the sports colours, which my mum sewed onto to my blazer and 35 years later I still have it!

Sharon Treadway

This team photo shows the girls in yellow tops. One girl has her badges sewn onto her shorts, and one girl has full colours sewn onto her blazer.

Students who did well at sports were awarded 'colours', which had to be stitched onto their blazers. Half colours were worn around the cuffs, and full colours went round the collar as well. As I remember, it was red for football, white for cricket and yellow for athletics.

Mary Rowan

I remember that we were all meant to get our uniform from Marks & Spencer. One girl bought her trousers from another shop, and sewed in the label from her blouse so the teachers wouldn't find out. She got caught when a teacher looked at her trousers and asked "Bust 32?"

Carol French

Mr Neaves' Form Group, 4N taken in 1976. Mr Neaves taught English. Most girls now wear tights instead of socks.

During the 1970s the black wool blazer was replaced by a thin nylon blue one.

Kevin Summers

1980s

Prefects had a special badge on their blazers. I was the Ash Bus Prefect.

Janet French

Boy's hair had to be short and above the collar line. I remember one boy having hair past the collar (not by much). He was excluded from school until he had his hair cut. In support of him, about half the school sat on the field in protest at him having to have his hair cut. The protest did not unfortunately make any difference and the pupil still had to have his hair cut. This would also apply for hair that was too short (shaved).

Stella Leitner

Mr Elliot in a lighter moment, modelling school cap

Lower School uniform in 1982, as worn by Mr Boorman's class

Miss lePage's class wear the Upper School uniform (1982)

1990s

Ties were red for the lower school with a stripe, and blue for the upper school with little red shields on. If you were a prefect you had a red stripe across your tie.

Anon

2000s

The upper school ties changed so that the shields were pale blue instead of red and students were allowed to wear polo shirts in the summer term.

Inspirational Staff

1930s

Twelve teachers started at the school in 1935: Mr Taylor, Mr Turner, Mr Hopper, Mr Davey, Mr Blogg, Mr Bonning, Miss Jackson, Miss Foord, Miss Harle, Miss Dawe, Miss Robson and Miss Brann. The caretaker was Mr Strentfield.

Editor

Mr Cook, an outstanding Head, and Mr Hyde, a wonderfully inspiring English teacher, both told me, knowing my disappointment at not going to school in Dover, that it was not the building that counted but the effort that I put into my education. They were a real inspiration and full of encouragement. They told us all that whatever we chose to do in life we could do it if we were prepared to work. Such words from respected teachers were an inspiration towards succeeding.

Miss Brann was Head of Girls at the time. If you had so much as a curl that shouldn't be there or a hat that was tilted at the wrong angle you would be up before her.

Mr Hopper, our geography teacher, was very handsome – he looked like Clark Gable and was admired by all the girls!

Eirwen Richards

Claire Herrington, writing in 1985, remembers her Uncle Bob (Robert Collard) who started at the school in 1935 talking about his science teacher Mr Taylor blowing up the lab!

Editor

1940s

Mr Cook was the Head Master throughout my time at school and everyone liked him. I remember his long stride that allowed him to cover the ground quickly, so surprising you with his appearance in the playground. Not that we did anything wrong!

Ivan Beer

Mr Rosseter was my favourite teacher. He was a gem. He often came out with little sayings. One statement he made was "Empires come and Empires go, but you will live to see the British Empire gone and be no more." I thought to myself, I cannot believe that …

He had over his blackboard a model of Richborough Castle, Eastry Parish Church, and Medieval houses all made by pupils before the war and preserved until he came back.

Mr Fright was the PE teacher – he had just come out of the army as a PT Instructor.

David Parfitt

Mr Fright with his class in 1943

I remember Mrs Maloney very well. One day she hit me in class, so I stood up and hit her back!

Valerie Hopper

Mr Clarke came to the school to teach woodwork, but changed to teach metalwork when Mr Blogg came to the school. Mr Blogg was a good teacher, my husband still has a three-legged milking stool made from a piece of ash that came from Ash and a nice book stand.

Joyce Parfitt

Miss Chidwick taught us cookery. At the end of the lessons we had to clean up and one day it was my turn to clean the cooker. When Miss Chidwick came past and told me to 'use some gumption, girl' I scrubbed harder - I didn't realise that she meant Gumption, the cleaning paste!

Maureen Peattie

The headmaster was Mr Cook, who tolerated being called 'Cookie'. He lived in the house beside the school.

Maureen Cullen

Miss Newman was the biology teacher. She was a very excitable and enthusiastic person, and loved to take us on nature walks to the Worth streams. She also kept bees at the school.

Mr Wicks lived in Deal, and cycled every day – he taught Current Affairs and was a very pleasant man. Miss Plumber was the art teacher when I first arrived, then Mr Abraham took over.

David Parfitt

Students/staff could buy the honey that was produced in the hives.

Editor

Mr Cook would wander round with his hands behind his back and his glasses on his head, asking 'Has anyone seen my glasses?'

Valerie Dodd

The staff in 1947, now increased to 19 plus the headmaster.

Back Row: Mr Sage, Mr Clarke, Mr Cowell, Mr Fox, ?, Mr Walker, Mr Rosseter, Mr Blogg, Mr Hopper, Mr Abraham, Mr Fright

Seated: Mrs Blogg, Mrs Cooper, Miss Jackson, Mr Cook, Mrs Warwick, Mrs Gill, Mrs Clarke,

Seated: Mrs Fielder, Miss Newman

I remember Mr Cook, the headmaster, Art – Mrs Dawe, Music/English/Maths – Mrs Jackson, Biology – Miss Newman, PE – Miss Foord.

Barbara Pope

1950s

The gardening shed lay between the girls' playground and the HORSA Huts. My first gardening master's name escapes me, as he was known by all as "Dibber." He came by this name due to hitting my friend "Goggs" over the head with one in the shed! Dibber was followed by a very different kettle of fish, Mr. Everard. He was big, ex Royal Navy, and HATED all boys. He constantly SHOUTED. One day the class hard case, "Shimmer" asked him, why? We thought he was for the chop, but Mr. Everard knelt down to Shimmer's level, and said "Because if I shout you will LISTEN!!!!!!!" We did!

Andrew Frost

The teachers I remember are:

Mr Hopper – geography
Mr Wickes - english
Mr Desborough – gardening
Miss Chidwick – cooking
Miss Newman – biology
Mrs Gill – craft
Mr Rossetor – R.I. and history
Miss Williams/Mrs Austin – games

Sylvia Moseley

Our 2nd year teacher in class B.1. was Mr Rosseter (known as Beaky for his prominent facial feature) who was known for his accuracy with a piece of chalk on those who were not paying attention.

Francis Butler

"Beaky" Rosseter was the History and RI master. He was also known as "The Rose Eater." He came to school on a "sit up and beg" bike that he rode in a very stiff and upright manner. "RI" was interpreted by us as "Ridiculous Ideas."

Andrew Frost

The staff in 1952, photographed in the quad.

Back row – Mr Wicks, Mr Desborough, Mr Rosseter, Mr Merriman, Mr Goodburn, Mr Martin, Mr Portman, Mr Hayes, Mr Sharp, Mr Abraham

Seated - Miss May, Mrs Gill, Miss Chidwick, Mr Cook, Miss Newman, Mrs Crouch, Mrs Cooper, Mrs Howard-Jones

Front - Mr Fox, Mr McQueen, Mr Blogg

Mr. Cook. People who didn't know him probably get tired of those who of us who did constantly going on about him. *Had* they known him, they would understand why we do it. I first came into close touch with him in the school choir. I was not interested in singing, but did love music. I liked to hear the choir rehearsing, and would sit outside the gym listening. One day he pulled me in, literally, and I found myself a member. I soon found that all the songs that so affected me were by the same composer, Schubert. Mr. Cook loved Schubert too, and we were friends from that day. The choir was his baby; he was choirmaster and accompanist. He was a very good and enthusiastic pianist. I can see him now, crouched over the piano, eyeing us, ready to go! No, no, NO! Rhythm, RHYTHM!!

Don't squeeze it out like toothpaste! TA, ta ta ta, TA, ta ta ta - attack it!

He had been to Harrow School, so one of our songs was "Forty Years On." There was one awful dirge we had to sing. It stood out like a sore thumb from the rest of our music, "Non nobis domine." Feeling brave one day, I asked him why we sang it. "Well, its like this, Frost. Miss Plum likes it". Enough said. I assume that she was something to do with the school governors.

Andrew Frost

I remember standing outside the headmaster's study at the end of the lunchtime recess waiting for a caning. Standing outside was the more painful of this exercise as the rest of the school filed past and gloated! In retrospect, the teaching staffs were excellent, with some instilling the fear of God but also a high standard of learning.

Ron Brown

I think my favourite teacher was a Mr. Clarke who was the metalwork teacher and who also ran the school cricket teams, both of which I enjoyed.

One of my favourite memories was a time in P.T when Mr Fox, taking the class, accepted a challenge to a one-on-one cricket ball catching competition when the first one to drop the ball received the "slipper". It wasn't me so my claim to fame was to give punishment to a teacher - I think he was a good sport.

Bernard Rogers

When it was the Coronation, Mr Rosseter the History teacher made a huge papier mache crown – it was very impressive!

Myrna Petley

I remember Mr Fox who taught PE in the late 1950. He used to take the detentions, and he was a dab hand with the size 10 slipper!

David Stone

If we were slow in changing for PT Mr Fox would make us do it outside, no matter how cold it was.

Brian Wilmshurst

Other ex-pupils remember Mr Fox as being a bit of a heartthrob – Editor

Our metalwork teacher was Mr Clarke, a lovely man, rather stout, but an enthusiastic cricketer with a fizzing round-arm fast bowl at net practice.

Glynn Tucker

The metalwork room during the 1950s

Mr. Clark taught metal work. When I started, there was a partly-built steam loco in the shop. Rumour had it that it had been started when the school opened. It looked exactly the same when I left in 58!

Mr. Clark was a jolly old chap. I got on with him because we both loved classical music, as well as engineering history. He also loved cricket - we differed on that. He had a VERY low opinion of women, and too high an opinion of the qualities of Vienna boys choir, we felt.

Andrew Frost

Miss Austin, who taught PE during the 1950s

tudents in 1956, girls in front and boys behind.

Who can forget "mucker" Merriman the science teacher? I seem to remember that his hands were always a very deep shade of brown - something to do with potassium nitrate?

Anon

Mr Merriman was also known as 'my-two-sons' Merriman, as this was a favourite saying of his. - Editor

In addition to these, pupils remember:

Mrs Cooper – English handwriting
Mr Sharp – music
Mr Hayes – science and practical drawing
Mr Goodburn – craft e.g. bookbinding
Mr Abrahams – art
Mr Robinson – PE and games
Miss Dawkins - dancing

Miss Newman taught biology. She looked after the bees. The hives were at the far side of the sports field, over a fence in an adjoining field. She was always trying to get us interested, but didn't have much luck!

I have no idea how much truth there is in this, but those who claimed to have been there at the time swore it is true. Before the new library as built, Mr. Wicks taught in one of the HORSA huts. The huts being at the back of the school, he used the rear entrance, and parked his car by the field. On one foggy winter afternoon, a group of boys surrounded the car, picked it up, and carried it out into the middle of the field. No one now has any idea how thick fog could be in those pre clean air act days, and the story may well be true.

Andrew Frost

1960s

Mr Wallace - Who could forget the reassuring thwack of a lump of conveyor belt rubber cut in the shape of a cricket bat smacked on the desk to shut us up. As a technical drawing teacher he had no equal, and as a 5th year form teacher we got away with murder (well, dismantling the school electrics anyway!)

Bernard Watson

Mr Gleedle the TD teacher was known as 'Glum' Gleedle. He was known for throwing the board rubber or even a pair of compasses to attract the attention of a daydreaming pupil.

Anon

Miss Chidwick taught us Domestic Science. We had to learn how to iron and fold a hanky perfectly before we were allowed to move on to other things!

Brenda Elgar

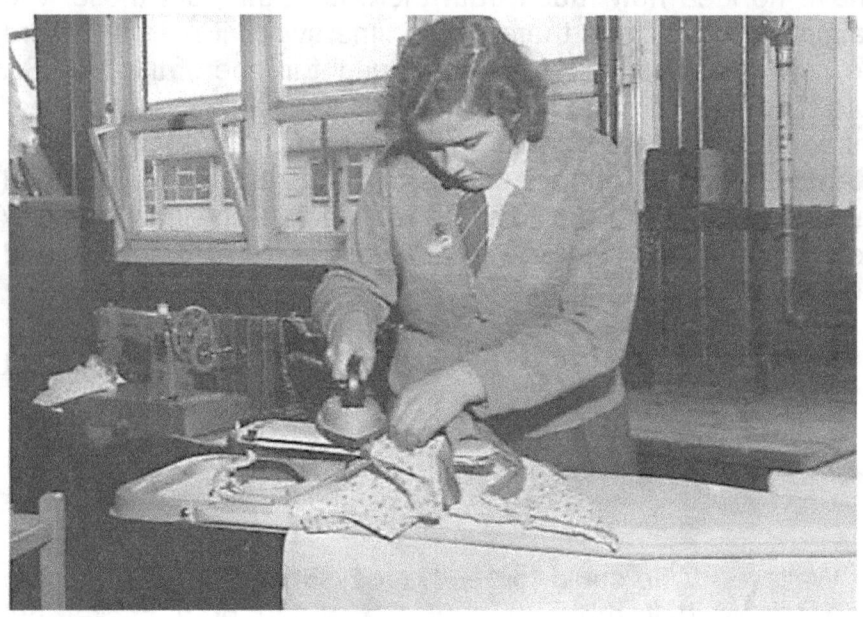

1970s

Mr Probert: what a lovely man. Thanks to him I can grow all my own veg. Miss Le Page was my form teacher. Miss Greenwood - well what can I say - she taught me to sew but she put the fear of god into me.

Anon

I was Head Girl during my last year, which gave me a closer relationship with many of the teachers, especially Mr Gilbert and Miss Greenwood, both of whom I always found to be firm but fair, with just the right amount of authority and an all important sense of humour.

Freda Francis

'Percy' Probert taught Rural Studies and always insisted on opening the doors whilst we attended assembly, come rain snow or howling gale!

Mr Burnand teaching ceramics outside the art rooms

Mr. Burnand was the Art Teacher who started my love of all things creative. I remember being given one of his pottery figures at end of term – I kept it for years.
I also remember Mr. Wallace (Wally), Technical Drawing. Brilliant teacher of TD, but we all lived in fear of 'The Bat'! A rather hard lump of leather applied to posteriors of wayward boys. Someone eventually 'kidnapped' 'The Bat'!................... Steven! Was that you?

Paul Isemonger

Mr. Wicks the English teacher instilled in me a love of reading and taught me NEVER to waste time and always carry a book with me, which I do to this day!

Linda Ridden

Miss Greenwood was the sewing teacher. We made long skirts one year, and pinafores another year.

Carol Coleman

Miss Williams not only taught PE but was also the 'dreaded one' when on dinner duty in the canteen. She made you eat every single morsel, including the fat and gristle! You did not move from that table until you had done so. All the kids sitting at that table were not allowed to leave until ALL plates were empty .... needless to say, a few hankies were full of food to be emptied into the bins at a later time!

I have to say that in my time at the school I remember Mr Wicks, head of English who was an inspiration, and Mr Fox, who believed in me and encouraged me. Great teachers.

Terence Sharp

I had an excellent five years at school and I loved every minute of it. The teachers I remember well are Mrs Dalkin, the PE teacher, Miss Humphreys, cooking and Mr Limbrick, gardening.

Anon

Mr. Wickes, English...wicked sense of humour and a fondness for the dramatic. Gimlet eyes with Gandalf eyebrows with a fantastic military moustache! Gave me a deep love of Shakespeare. Insisted that the boys should walk upright with one hand half in, half out of pocket. He would stop you in playground to adjust your stance!

Mrs. Mallard, Fencing Coach started me on a lifelong love of the sport. Still fence today.

Paul Isemonger

Some of the staff in 1973 after a hockey match against fifth year students. Mr Dean, Mr Probert, Mr Boorman, Mr Dunn, Ms Nutly, Ms lePage, ?, Mr Clapman, Ms Laneham, Mr Hedges, Mrs Pert.

Miss Greenwood would watch you getting off the bus and say "Go and wash your faces, girls"

Carol French

My favourite subjects were English, biology with Mrs. Franks who nurtured my love of nature and wild life then history with Mrs. Way who filled my imagination with stories of our past both from this country and other parts of the world.

The teachers I had have all affected me in some way or another, Miss Pocket the librarian, Mr. Probert rural studies, Mr. Fox my first year form teacher, Mr. Styles my second year form teacher, Mrs. Stanard domestic science, Miss Greenwood fashion, Mrs. O'Neill drama, Mr. Dixon English, Miss LePage PE, Miss Quickenden PE, the three men who taught woodwork, metalwork, maths and PE who always used to walk around together(I may not remember their names at this precise moment, but I can see their faces still quite clearly in my mind!),

Mr. Barnard art, Mr. Gilbert Headmaster, Mr. Hopper Deputy Headmaster, Mrs. Manning French and Mrs. Priddle French.

I sincerely owe these teachers a debt of gratitude for the knowledge that they imparted to me and I shall never forget them............. no matter how hard I try!!!

Linda Ridden

Mrs. Way was a quirky and cool history/form teacher. Can trace my love of history and the consequent published books back to her enthusiasm for the subject. Top treat – listening to her 'hippy' stories.

Paul Isemonger

The science block under construction in 1973

Mr Rosseter also taught my father when he attended Sandwich School in the 1940s. He was our religious instruction teacher and we always had a test at the end of the week with ten questions. Most times I would have all ten right, but would absolutely *never* be given 10/10. I asked why this was, and he replied that no-one is perfect and there was always room for improvement. Fair comment, but oh the injustice of it! It was the same for the duration of his time at school, even when my father was there!

Linda Ridden

Some of the other teachers remembered by students from the 1970s are:

Mr Hilton	Mrs Franks
Mr Fisher	Mr Easton
Mrs Furnival	Mr Hedges
Mrs Shanks	Mr Moore
	Mr.Chapman

1980s

Students remember the following teachers from the 1980 :

Miss Dalkin – PE
Mr Limbrick – gardening
Miss Humphreys – cooking
Miss Greenwood – sewing
Mrs Stannard – domestic science
Mr Dixon – history
Mr James

formal picture of the staff in 1980

A less formal picture of some of the younger staff (1980)
Mr Aldred, Mr Rabray, Mr Flowers
Mrs Bragger, Miss Stevens, Mrs Read, Miss lePage

1990s

Does anyone remember how Mr Marshall would start a lesson (CDT) but his fire brigade pager would go off and then you would see him running to his car and off like Steve McQueen in *'Bullet'*.

Brad Head

I remember Mrs Osbourne. A really nice lady as well. Sadly like Mrs Linkin, Mrs Powell, and Mr Kilmurray she found out that trying to teach me anything about the French language was a waste of time!

Anon

I remember Mr Elliot, the Headmaster. He was mostly serious and strict, but what I mostly remember him for was once jumping into a skipping rope being turned by two people at break, to the amazement of everyone watching!

Anon

2000s

I remember Mr Howe used to teach PE. I was really bad at the javelin, and one day he stood in front of me and shouted "Just aim for me!" I don't think he expected me to throw it as hard as I did that time.... Years later, I met him in a pub and I asked him to join our darts game. He agreed, saying "But this time, I'm going to stand behind you!"

Stephen Smith

My favourite memory is of Mr Ouertani – he was a brilliant form tutor and a fantastic bloke. When I first met him, he was a small, greying, middle aged Tunisian man... who really liked Slipknot and heavy metal music! He was really good with the kids and knew how to have a tongue-in-cheek joke with us. I could go on and on, such as when we took a picture of him at a strange angle, and he uncannily represented a totem pole. Hope to see him out and about sometime soon so I can buy him a beer.

Simon Harris

I remember when I was in yr 7 English our teacher (I can't remember his name, he was great - an older man with big hair who walked with a limp , terrifying but friendly at the same time) anyway he was reading Roald Dahl's 'Boy' to us and it was the part where Roald describes having his tonsils taken out and our teacher was so graphic and emotive he actually made me feel sick!

Oh and as if I could forget favourite teacher, Mrs Peel. She was great - I loved her class and her so kind and loving and would do anything for her pupils - one of the best teachers I've ever had!

Ben Nuttall 2006

Many students will remember Mrs Tutton as their PE teacher or as Head of Year. She is now one of the school's Deputy Head Teachers

The scariest teacher was Mr Shardlow, who was the deputy headmaster.

Philip Rowcroft

Lessons

1930s

My form teacher was Mr Hyde, a brilliant English teacher. I can still hear him reciting John Mansfield's 'Sea Fever'! He was not above flicking boys behind the ears if they misbehaved or were inattentive.

Miss Dawes was our art teacher. She gave me an assignment to design a wardrobe for a lady who had an invitation to visit a country house from Friday evening to Sunday afternoon. I had to design an evening dress, a golf outfit, a cocktail dress, a ball gown and an outfit for a luncheon party. I still have the designs up in my attic somewhere.

One science lesson consisted of a visit to a stream. We crossed over the Deal Road and across a meadow and a stream ran through to Sandwich. We all took a jam jar, collected water and went back to school and looked at drops of water under a microscope. I could never forget the surprise I felt when I saw that water had 'skin' or the look of a water boatman.

Mr Davey, a very handsome young man, took science with the boys. We always had separate lessons and our nearest to sex education was plant reproduction! I was probably twelve when I learned where babies came from!

If we wrote a good story or poem or anything of note it could go in the anthology - it was quite an honour to have work entered in the anthology.

Eirwen Fletcher

Mr Davey in 1937. Note the veranda on the left, which was later filled in and now houses student lockers.

Apart from the academic side, the girls had domestic science, needlework, the boys did carpentry and metalwork, also music and art were high on the list.

Sports played a large part of our lessons, both indoors and out, we had a team for hockey, netball and rounders and the boys a football team, also high jump, long jump and much more and a well-equipped gym.

Grace Wray

1940s

In PE the girls did hockey, netball and rounders and the boys did football, cricket and rugby. When we had to do PE indoors, the four houses had to line up in a row to do 'physical jerks'. The team leaders, myself included, stood in the front.

Dennis Parsons

Mr Clark was the metalwork teacher. He and Mr Cook were the only male teachers who stayed throughout the war. Mr Clark was quite old but very patient, showing us how to make tools for the garden.

David Parfitt

Sport was my main interest and I played cricket, football and table tennis for the school. Mr Clarke was the metalwork teacher and he also took us for cricket. I once took a fantastic catch going high over my head, fielding a short mid-off. All I got from Mr Clarke was "That was a bit of luck".

Ivan Beer

The metalwork room in 1947

I enjoyed the cooking and sewing classes. Another activity I enjoyed was the dancing classes where I learnt to do the Sailor's Hornpipe.

Barbara Pope

We didn't have homework. All our schoolwork stayed firmly in our desks with the inkwells and the ledge for the pen.

Ivan Beer

Class 4Ag with Mr Probert centre front

1950s

Mr Probert taught gardening. I seem to remember as much mud throwing as gardening during those lessons!

Michael Cowell

The one thing that sticks in my mind even to this day is going into Mr Rossetor's class for History and seeing over the blackboard the saying Read Mark Learn and Inwardly Digest, the times over the years I have tried to drill it into my offspring!

Anthea Croucher

Boxing in 1954

When it was wet and we couldn't go outside to do PE they took us to the hall to do ballroom dancing. If we refused we were sent to Mr Gilbert

Michael Cowell

Class D1 in 1954. These students would be in the current Year 10.

I was very happy there and really enjoyed working on the school allotments, which was for one lesson per week - not enough for lots of us.

Stewart Watson

The school had a 2-ton horse roller, which they used to roll the cricket pitches. On the day in question, Mr Fox gave eight of us the job of using it, which involved four of us pulling and four pushing it backwards and forwards. For those pulling it was necessary to lean back with all of our weight to stop it and get it moving in the opposite direction. At the time, I was pulling with all of my strength when I fell flat onto my back and I instantly knew that there was no way that the others were going to stop the roller before it went over my legs. Fortunately, I threw my legs up over my head into a backward roll and the roller struck me hard against my pelvis.

As soon as Mr Fox realised that an accident had occurred he literally sprinted across the field, whisked me up into his arms and carried me to the headmaster's office. I was taken to Deal hospital and was told that if I had been any older I would almost certainly have broken my back.

My accident obviously made its mark on the school because in about 1985 when I was the Chief Inspector of Police at Dartford I discovered that one of my constables went to the school about 12 years later than me. I asked him if the school had a horse roller on the sports field when he was there. "Yes", he said, "but old Foxy wouldn't let any of us get anywhere near it because a boy had been seriously injured by it in the past." He couldn't believe it when I replied, "I was that boy!"

Patrick Gleeson

Cookery in the 1950s. Each girl had to make their own hat and pinafore in Sewing before they could join in the Cookery classes.

I joined the school choir in order to get out of geography. The Headmaster came to hear us sing and asked me if I had joined the choir for this reason. (Presumably he was not impressed with my singing). He drew a map on the board and asked me to point to a certain country, which I could not do, so I was told to go to geography and not to the choir.

Doreen Anderson

The boiler room was under the needle work/science rooms and on the chimneystack was the bell that controlled the school day, breaks and lesson changes, and at five to twelve it sent the waiters to the canteen. In the event of the bell not working there was a heavy steel plate, about 6" wide and 18" deep, and a length of steel to hit it with, hanging from the edge of the veranda outside the needle work room.

Andrew Frost

The veranda adjoining the quad.
The end classroom was at one time the year 11 common room.

In the third year our form teacher was Mr Wickes, a dapper, moustached figure with a fierce reputation. He was probably quite a kindly man but that was not always apparent. The main memory of that year was the dreaded lecturettes, one in each term, in which you had to speak about a subject for ten minutes and then take questions on it for another five minutes.

Glyn Tucker

My main memory of Sports Day (or was it Open Day?) is the of the Fancy Dress competition. A lot of work went into this. The judges were the needlework mistress and Mr Rosseter. It was a serious competition, and the prize went to the best costume, there was seldom any dissent from the onlookers.

Mr. Cook never took a class officially, but would stand in now and again for the odd missing teacher. He would come into class and say, "Now, what lesson is this?" He knew quite well what it was! Someone would say "Geography, Sir." "What have you been studying?" "The grain-growing areas of Canada, Sir." "Oh dear, I don't like the sound of that. Let's see if you have learnt anything really important. Where is Timbuktu?" Laughter! "There's no such place, Sir!" "Yes there is! Get your atlases out!" And a marvellous half-hour of general knowledge questions would follow.

Andrew Frost

In the greenhouse

I remember rote learning of the Kings and Queens of England, attending music classes, rote learning spelling,

Ron Brown

Each year, fifth year students showed the dresses they had made in Needlework class.

I remember Science lessons. In the science lab, we used to take syrup tins, make a hole in the top, fill them with gas and light the gas so that the lids would ping off and hit the ceiling just as Mr Merriman started his lesson!

I also remember Mr Clark who was the metal work teacher. He did out-of-hours cricket lessons even though he was short and portly - he was a very good slow bowler who taught many of us the good tricks of the trade, which stood me in good stead during my service life. Also, if we wore loose clothing in the metal work classroom and it got caught in any of the machinery, he was very quick with a pair of scissors!

Brian White

There was a weekly spelling competition. Each day we were given five spellings and on Friday's we were tested.

Brian Wilmshurst

1960s

Needlework is a very interesting subject, though it is not so interesting at school as it is at home. At school if the teacher is giving you a lecture on something that you know how to do, then that is where the trouble starts. You fidget with your pencil or annoy your neighbour and then get told off. Then when you start working again, and you've done some machining the teacher comes up and says "That is crooked; you'll have to undo that." Then you get mad.

Sylvia Moseley, writing in 1961 as a 2nd year.

I remember that my friends and I always ran together in cross-country. One year, the mistress made all four of us start at different times – we still finished together, though, so she gave up and let us be Score Keepers instead!

Brenda Elgar

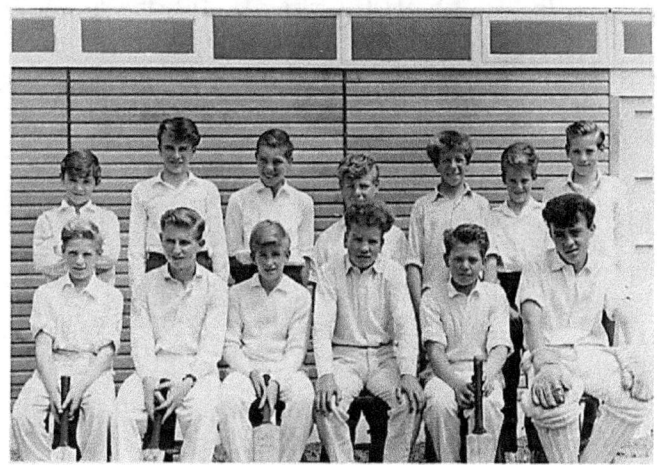
The cricket team of 1963

I enjoyed my school life very much with Maths and Domestic Science being my best subjects. Miss Chidwick was my Domestic Science teacher and even to this day I think of the way she taught us the basics in cookery. I'm pleased to say that with that knowledge I was able to make both my daughters' and granddaughters' three tier wedding cakes.

Patricia King

1970s

I still have certificates for sporting events. In 1964, I received netball colours, which if I remember correctly were half colours - therefore the coloured bands went round the blazer sleeves in the colour of your house, which meant mine were red.

In 1965 I received full colours, which meant the colour was round the collar of your blazer as well. Many netball and hockey games were played; my position in netball was goal shooter. Gymnastics were performed to parents in the quadrangle.

Julie Rogers

I remember Mr. Gilbert, the Headmaster, used his army revolver to start sports day races! Top treat - being asked to collect said revolver from the Office and bring out to Mr. Gilbert on the sports field! Somehow I think that wouldn't happen today!

Paul Isemonger

We made raspberry buns and ginger biscuits in Cooking, and we still use the Christmas cake recipe to this day!

Freda Francis

I still have my exercise books from the sewing classes and our first item to make was a cookery apron in yellow Gingham. I made several dresses and only recently threw out the patterns of some I made in class, including a Mary Quant dress pattern with smocking across the bust line. I also have some embroidered dressing table mats that I did in class.

Julie Rogers

In my first year Mr. Fox held a boxing tournament for all the boys to take part in and I can remember the thrill and excitement of being a part of this tournament. Although I wasn't boxing myself, I knew by sight or even personally all the boys that were taking part in the tournament, which made me actually feel part of it too.

Linda Ridden

John Lelliot winning the cross country in 1960 for Ash House.

Cross country. Wow what amazing fun! All six of us set off at a cracking pace. Five minutes outside of school, kit off, straight into river for a half-hour of wild splashing. Quick sun-bathe. Back into clothes, take the short cut to arrive two minutes or so before due time, wet hair plastered across forehead and feigned heavy breathing. Collapse at feet of PE master. "Well done boys! Working up a good sweat! That's the ticket!"

Boxing! It hurt!...... a lot! Okay bit of lateral thinking needed here. First experience of school Boxing competition. Pay opponent all your pocket money not to hit me very hard! " I will take a dive" is the conspiratorial conversation. The day of the competition arrives, feeling pleased with my subterfuge. Round One, He hit me very, very hard. I fall down semi-conscious. He kept my money.

Forged sick notes to get out of Boxing. Half hour of sitting on a pile of smelly leather Boxing gloves in the dim light of the sports shed with my good mate 'Prune'. Subject of conversation? Latest Test score? Looking forward to the Rugby season? Nope just.... girls girls girls! Oh, and Monty Python... and the Man from U.N.C.L.E.... bubble gum cards.... air guns.......

Fencing! Fantastic! Sign me up! I get out of Boxing. Two boys eight girls! Life felt good.

Paul Isemonger

In 1970 a group of 2nd year students were given a plot of wild land, behind the canteen area. The idea was to conserve the wildlife, flowers and trees that were naturally there. We catalogued the area and planted plants and trees that were sympathetic to the area and create a walkway through this natural area for all to enjoy. It was a part of a national campaign 'Conservation year 1970' to conserve our natural landscape. The work was recorded and organised by the junior school science teacher on 8mm cine film and was show on open days. I was a big part of the exercise.

Terence Sharp

Working in the greenhouse in the summer of 1973

1980s

The teacher we all thought of as a bit of a heartthrob was Mr Aldred, who taught PE.

Lisa Powell

Mr Aldred in 1990.

When someone did well in sports, their name was put onto a brass plaque and put up round the school hall.

Janet French

Food Technology in the room adjoining the quad.

Lessons included much the same as today with information technology just being introduced and separate science lessons consisting of Biology, Physics and Rural Science. Sewing was also a lesson together with Home Economics. Not only did both girls and boys learn how to cook, but how to iron and change a plug. I really enjoyed Rural Science lessons. I can remember learning how to take cuttings from geraniums.

Stella Leitner

1990s

Also when I started there it was a sort of pupil garden in the middle I grew some vegetables there and if I recall there were chickens down the side of the dinner hall

Brad Head

Rural Science was still being taught in 1992 when Mrs Copsey was employed as Horticultural Technician.

Editor

Technology was used increasingly during the 1990s

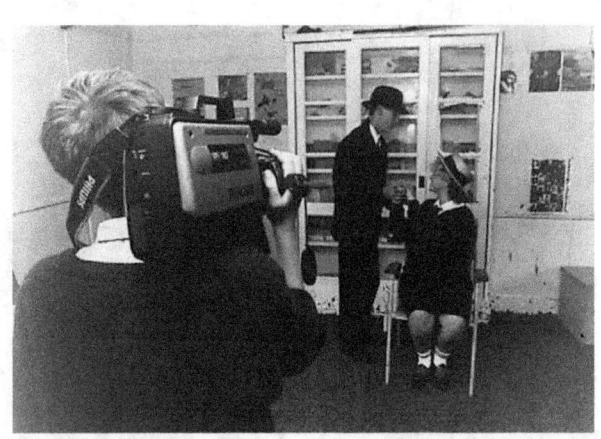

2000s

I organised a trip to Thorpe Park in the sixth form for our Leisure & Recreation course – we were the last year to do this course. The teachers were Mrs Tutton, Mr Pallant and Mrs Edwards.

Philip Rowcroft

Mr Pallant, Head of PE

Sports Day is still a chance to pupils to compete for inter-house trophies.

School Dinners

Inside the original wooden canteen. This photograph was taken in 1935

1930s

I remember Miss Jackson sitting at the head of our table at lunch (I believe all the teachers took turns to sit at the head of each dining table) and she said to one girl "Not eating your cabbage, Betty?" Betty didn't like cabbage, but Miss Jackson watched as she devoured the lot!

Eirwen Fletcher

In the canteen the tables were properly laid for lunch, with clean, laundered table-cloths, cutlery and glasses. The boy waiters wore ample aprons and the girls wore pleasant waitress's caps. Everyone stood for Grace to be said, a two-course meal followed and there was opportunity for everyone to learn some polite and considerate table manners.

Mr Rosseter reminiscing in 1985

Canteen staff pictured in 1937

1940s

School dinners were 2 shillings and 3 pence a week. They were fine and we were appointed lunch monitors to wait on the teachers. I cannot think of any bad incidents of food poisoning!

Ivan Beer

The staff sat on a table in the middle of the hall and prefects served the meals. Students sat down and the prefects carried the meals out on trays.

Maureen Pettie

At this time, senior and junior students were seated separately

Editor

As regarding school lunches, these were plentiful and good.

Barbara Pope

Sometime during 1943 the school canteen was brought into operation. Senior children were made responsible for service in the canteen – and their duties consisted of preparation and waiting on tables, serving food and clearing the trolleys.

Miss Newman writing in 1985

1950s

By 1950, the canteen was serving 800 meals a day, catering for the 650 students at the school plus those at the Junior School.

Editor

I loved school dinners and looked forward to dinnertime for the cheese-potato salad, the flapjacks and cream and lots more.

Doreen Anderson

The canteen in 1958

The Canteen was segregated, boys at the school end, girls the other, separated by the plate scrapers. They cleaned the plates brought to them by the waiters. We prefects had our own table between the girls and boys end, and, if my memory serves me correctly, the boys and girls dined together.

Andrew Frost

The school canteen was run with the help of pupils. You would volunteer to help with waiting on the tables, serving the meals or working on the trolleys clearing the dirty plates etc.

The canteen was divided into two halves, boys one end and girls the other end. Staff had a table in the middle. The tables were covered with white tablecloths and Mr Cook said we and one other school were the only schools to have tablecloths. The canteen helpers wore white aprons. A bell would ring at 11.50am for the staff to go and lay up the tables ready for lunch, which was split into two sittings.

Meals cost sixpence a day, payable on Monday. The menu was a set meal, but there were good. Steak & kidney pie, rabbit pie, roast beef, one day would be salad with mashed potato and cheese flan. The puddings could be rice, tapioca, chocolate sponge with chocolate sauce, jelly and cream (known as 'soap suds'), or marmalade pudding and custard.

Brian Wilmshurst

1960s

Pupils served the school meals on a roster basis, and we had two sittings.

Sylvia Moseley

'Dinner Ladies' photographed in the 1960s

1970s

Nearly everyone had school dinners, gypsy tart being a big favourite!

Sharon Crowley

The old wooden canteen served the school until 2006, when it was demolished.

Shirley Taylor remembers buying dinner tickets in the 1970s. These were later replaced by tokens and eventually phased out in the 1990s

Editor

I used to hate giving up my valuable time to eat! Looking back we had really great meals. I always gave my Gypsy Tart away, still can't stand it. Used to eat everyone else's veg and pies. Fond memories of lumpy custard or chocolate sauce! Happy days,

Linda Ridden

1980s

In the 1980s Margaret Thatcher's Conservative government ended entitlement to free meals

All first years got had the responsibility of 'slops'. In the old canteen which was situated in the Dover Road, Girl's playground 2 pupils had to stand with 'Cling film' like aprons on and scrape everyone's food left-over's into a slop bucket.

Stella Leitner

1990s

2000s

I remember that the Year 7 students had to do the slops in the canteen on a rota basis. Luckily the system stopped before I had to take a turn.

Mark Jarrett

Breakfasts were introduced in 2006, and in 2009 the school was granted Healthy Schools status. The new restaurant continues to provide high-quality, locally sourced food.

Editor

In 2005 Year 10 students took part in a Challenge Week sponsored by Tilmanstone Salads.

Prefects and Monitors

1930s

There were prefects who stood in the corridors and outside the canteen to check that hands were washed before lunch and also to help with the serving of the meals.

Grace Wray

We had prefects in the corridors as we filed out in single file to breaks. Anyone stepping seriously out of line was sent to Mr Cook, who would deal with them himself.

Eirwen Fletcher

Prefects in 1938 with Mr Hyde

1950s

Mr. Cook was a cricket fan. I remember the display of cricketing history put on for him in the foyer of the new hall when he retired. Before the new hall was built, there was a scoreboard on the lawn at the edge of the boys playground. Am I remembering this correctly, did the prefects put up the latest test scores at break times? There was also a weather station there, a Stevenson Screen.

Andrew Frost

Students in 1959

The Head Boy was allowed to administer the slipper. Pupils who had done something wrong were allowed to choose whether they wanted to be slippered by the Head Boy or sent to the Headmaster. As I remember, none of them wanted to go to the Headmaster's room. Where did we do it? I think it was in the loo!

Anon

We still used what I understand are correctly described as metal dip pens and there were inkwells in the desktop and ink monitors to keep the inkwells filled.

In 1957 the new school library was opened, which was also our classroom, and I was appointed chief librarian with a staff of six girls. Among the challenges was learning the Dewey Decimal system to put the books in the right order. The memory of the smell of the boxes of new books and the pleasure of having the first choice stays with me to this day.

Glyn Tucker

Young Glyn Tucker seated bottom left with his form B1. the two students to his right are the form's milk monitors.

We had milk monitors who would get the milk for break time – 1/3 pint for each pupil.

Brian Wilmshurst

The school magazine of 1954 notes that each form had a Captain, a Vice-Captain, Librarians, Milk Monitors and a Blackboard Monitor.

Editor

Students from 1959

One thing I recall vividly was when I was made Head Girl. The badge I was given was silver with an enamel bulldog on the front; the Head Boy's was the same. The pin came loose on mine so I took it to Mr Cook who pinched it together with pliers. It wasn't long before I was left with just the pin only on my tie. After a sleepless night the next morning I went to Mr Cook with the pin and some pound notes as my mother said I was to offer to pay for a new one. Mr Cook was very understanding and said as they were especially made in Sheffield for the school, he couldn't replace it, so I was a Head Girl without a badge!

Patricia King

1960s

There were bus prefects & playground prefects.

John Durban

Prefects from 1967-8

John Martin was Head Boy 1963-4

1970s

None of the prefects wanted to do Playground duty – especially in the winter!

Freda Francis

In my fourth year I was given the job of Monitor, which I took very seriously and helped all the younger pupils walk around the corridor past Mr. Gilbert's Office to assembly, without talking. This coming from someone who couldn't ever stop talking at the best of times!

Then in my fifth year I rose to the giddy heights of Prefect and House Captain for Eastry House. I was just sooooo proud! I took my responsibilities very seriously and one day I kept back a young girl from my House who had been in trouble in the playground during morning break, and talked with her about her problems. (She seemed to settle down and became much happier after that which gave me a lovely warm glow inside to think that I'd actually been able to help her) I took her to her lesson and apologised for her lateness, which was ok, then I went to MY lesson and apologised for MY lateness, which was NOT ok! I was in deep doodoo with Miss Greenwood the fashion teacher and I had to do detention for being 10 minutes late to her lesson! Oh the unfairness of it all!

Linda Ridden

Mr Matthews with his student librarians

I remember being sent out of assembly for talking to my friend and having my prefects badge taken away for a month.

Anon

Mr Wickes was a Disciplinarian with a twinkle in his eye. First teacher to have enough faith in me to give me a position of responsibility by making me Bus Prefect. Doesn't sound much does it? but in a sea of under achieving it made all the difference to how I viewed my school life. It also gave me the chance to chat up the girls on the top deck! Think I missed out on the responsibility bit. Demoted to the ranks

Paul Isemonger

1980s

Prefects would line the corridors during class change over and at break times. One had to gain the privilege of being a prefect. The Prefects would ensure students walked in single file along the corridors and would knock bags of shoulders. In those days most boys bags for sports bags that would be slung over their shoulder however, they could potentially tear down work displays, hence why carrying them over their shoulder was not permitted.

No pupils where permitted into any of the school buildings during break and lunch time. It was the duty of the prefects to turn out any students.

Stella Leitner

Biology Lab Monitors in 1980

School Assemblies

Part of a whole school photograph taken in 1937

1950s

The three times per week in the morning we had school assembly, where I and another classmate were required to set-up and operate the back projector, used to project the words of the hymns onto a ground glass screen for the benefit of the senior school, who were assembled in the school hall/gym under the watchful and beady eye of the headmaster, George Cook (and woe betide anyone who didn't pay attention or sing!)

Ron Brown

We had assembly each morning, juniors at the front and seniors at the back and teachers around the sides. We would start with a piece of music e.g. The Hall of the Mountain King, Handel's Water Music etc, followed by Hymns, Prayers and any info we were required to know.

Brian Wilmshurst

This photograph, taken at an assembly in 2005, shows that the teachers still stand around the sides.

Assemblies were held in the old gym, the words of hymns were projected onto a screen, from behind, by a magic lantern. When we went into assembly, music would be playing from a 78rpm record, and projected on the screen would be a saying or quotation. Mr. Cook's favourite was "The man that hath no music in himself, nor is not moved by concord of sweet sound, is fit for treasons, stratagems and spoils. Let no such man be trusted."

Andrew Frost

1970s

I see that the school playground has now been built on. I do remember lining up there at the start of the day in our classes - shortest at the front graduating to tallest at the back and the marching to assembly. Do you still do that? - I jest

I also wonder if anyone remembers the School song, which was sung at the end of term assembly. The song started with - Lord dismiss us with thy blessing, once again assembled here..........

Terry Sharp

1980s

Assemblies would take place most mornings with sometimes a guest speaker on a Friday. Again boys and girls were separated with girls standing on one side of the hall and boys on the other. Quite frequently because of the length of time we had to stand, fainting occurred, me included.

At the end of every assembly the Head and Boys, Mr Hilton and the Head of Girls, Mrs Ferminger would carry out a uniform check on every student as they left the hall. If any item of uniform was not correct, then you would be pulled to one side and 'told off'.

Stella Leitner

The old gym/hall being dismantled in 1988. It was divided into two rooms to make a classroom and a library, and is now three classrooms.

I was very proud to be asked to sing solos in the assemblies, especially at Christmas time. I remember one year singing a modern carol duet with Ross Saxby and because I felt so proud, I was nearly in tears trying to sing it without letting my voice wobble. I still remember the words of that carol to this day!

Linda Ridden

The school hall laid out for the annual Chess Championships.

Clubs and Activities

1930s

The netball team with Miss Foord in 1938

1940s

Playing cigarette cards was one of the favourite games. The simple rules were to flick the cards towards a wall and the one nearest after ten throws picked up the pile. I confess to having two cards stuck together, which I kept back to the last throw, in case I was losing. The stiffened cards proved to be more accurate!

Ivan Beer

I played in the netball team, and my position was Shooter. We played in tournaments that included visiting other schools in the area, which I enjoyed very much.

Barbara Pope

A gym display from 1947, possibly on an Open Day.

Mr Fright loved to get us boys working on all the apparatus. One Open Days, he would train all the best boys to demonstrate to the visitors their skills.

David Parfitt

The Football team of 1944-45

The steps that were used by the glider club in the 1950s

1950s

The glider club was run by Mr Goodman, in his room which was between the gym and the road. (Now G5 – Ed) The school had a standardised glider. At lunch times they were flown from the top of the iron stairs that led down, on the outside of the building, from the second story of the front classroom block. They were trimmed to turn right, and fly down between the two-story block and the wooden science/wood work rooms.

Andrew Frost

The Glider Club in 1952

If none of us had any sweets we would play hangman in the cloakroom

Brian Wilmshurt

Girls who competed for England in 1949

Douglas Stone was the runner-up in the 1956 All-England Boxing Championships

My brother Colin and I were both members of the boxing club run by Mr Fox, a no-nonsense character in the great tradition of games masters.

One of my distinct memories is of the lingering smell of the sweaty boxing gloves as we ate the crisps saved from our packed lunch while waiting for the bus home.

I was also a narrow winner of a bout in the inter-house boxing tournament at which medals were presented by WWII fighter pilot hero Wing Commander Robert Stanford Tuck.

Ah, then there was the ballroom dancing club, run by Miss Williams, way ahead of Strictly ..... it's all coming back. My main memory, apart from the nervous trek across the floor to ask a girl to dance, was that we all had to have a folded handkerchief in our right hands to protect the girls' gowns from our sweaty embrace.

                                                            Glyn Tucker

I remember learning to set-up typeface and printing for the school magazine in the science lab.

Ron Brown

Country Dancing on the lawn,
now the site of two new science rooms

I was in the school netball team and used to go to school on Saturdays for netball.

Doreen Anderson

Fencing Club in the quad during July 1956

Sport I remember with affection - I represented the school in the discus. I was also in the school boxing team and was school champion at my weight. Mr Fox the sports master at the time nicknamed me "Slugger Watson". The matches were on a home and away basis and the coach drive to and from the matches was just great, full of banter with everyone supporting each other. Most of the lads came from Eastry Cottage Homes.

Stuart Watson

Helen Croucher's javelin record, set in 1953, has not yet been beaten.

I also remember lunchtime films of "Flash Gordon" being shown in the science classroom by Mr Merriman, which was popular.

Francis Butler

Mr Cook lived in a house adjoining the school grounds. I remember him saying in assembly one morning "I can understand you boys and girls wanting to get as far away from the school buildings as possible during a lovely warm dinner hour, but don't forget that the furthest you can get from the school puts you right against my garden fence. You would be AMAZED at some of the things I learn while having a quiet cup of tea in my garden at lunch time!"

Andrew Frost

1960s

1964 boys' gymnastics team

Does anybody else remember when we had to imagine a line down the field at playtime and girls were supposed to stay one side and boys the other, must have been in 1965, and how about the Black Panthers?

Myra Bullows

1964 netball team

During my time in Mr Merriman's class I was monitor responsible for the school 16mm film projector. I used to take it around to different classrooms and set it up for the teacher to show films. I also used to show lunchtime films during the winter in the science room; each session lasted about 25 minutes, showing such films as *'The 39 Steps'* and *'A Tale of Two Cities'* - these were serial films with the different episodes being sent to the school every week.

Fundraising barbeque in 1960

I think this picture was taken at a school fete in 1960. The location is at the rear of Mr Merriman's science class, the gas for the BBQ was from his class with a rubber tube passed out through a window - whatever would H&S say today!

I was only selling hot dogs at the BBQ, I don't think we had burgers back then, as you can see they were very cheap (only 6d each) and I had sold out.

John Durban

1970s

I remember the film shows that used to be put on in the school hall at lunch times by Mr Harlow in the mid to late 70's. For about 30p you got to see some really good school/pupil made films on the 'hi-tech' cine camera of the day.....IN COLOUR....... I still have, together with a few cast members, a copy of the Dracula Goes to School film staring Mr Probert getting killed in the greenhouse, and Mr Gilbert being eaten alive in his office...... great days eh.

Redmond McKinnon

We also had an end of term disco that year and they were always melodramatic and very exciting. In my first year it was so much fun to watch all the flirting going on between the older pupils, especially with the Head Boy and Head Girl as they were so much more grown up than us younger ones!

Linda Ridden

I remember taking home hamsters, rats, gerbils and mice for weekends and school holidays and following the eggs hatching in Mr Probert's class.

Sharon Crowley

It wasn't exactly part of the curriculum, but I remember that we used to nip down to The Blue Pigeons at Worth at lunchtimes!

Paul Southgate

Gym Club 1973

1980s

Fifth years had a common room which is somewhere near the end of the Peace Garden area/DT class. The room had a pool table, tape player and a tuck shop.

Stella Leitner

Nat West Bank brought a mobile bank van to the school at lunchtimes, and we could visit it to deposit our savings.

Marion Scott

1990s

Mr Martin, Head of Art in the 1990s, helped the GNVQ Art students to participate in Strange Cargo's annual Charivari event. This led to the formation of a street band, Brew-Ha-Ha!, and a series of Sandwich Street Carnivals.

Brew-Ha-Ha! Leading one of the Sandwich Street Festivals, with Big John in the background.

The 1997 Girls Hockey Team with Mrs Richardson, who was affectionately known as 'The Dragon'.

2000s

Year 8 Football Team 2005

Trips

1930s

Miss Jackson, our music teacher, took us to singing festivals at The Winter Garden Theatre in Margate, and I believe we were quite successful.

We went in to Sandwich to buy supplies for our cookery lessons - part of the training for good shopping habits! We were in full school uniform and expected to be polite and well behaved at all times. It all reflected on the school and it taught us loyalty and discipline.

Eirwen Fletcher

The school also visited Windsor and Hampton Court in 1935, and London Docks in 1939.

Editor

1940s

Students visited The Ideal Homes Exhibition in the 1940s, and The Chelsea Flower Show and the Ford works at Dagenham in 1948.

Editor

1950s

I remember that we went on a camping trip to Belgium

Douglas Tutton

When it was the Coronation, we all went to The Empire Cinema in Sandwich to watch a film of the ceremony.

I can remember going on a school trip to London Zoo and at sometime I can remember going on the River Thames. A school special train used to take us starting at Sandwich station. In those days it was a large steam engine that towed the train.

Rodney Betts

Students enjoying their lunch while at London Zoo

While in my third year, Mr Clark organised a trip to Fords of Dagenham and also I went again in my fourth year. The school was one of only two who were able to visit the factory because we could behave ourselves.

Brian WIlmshurst

The school returned several times to the Dagenham plant, including 1995 when a group of Year 11 students watched Ford Fiestas on the production line.

Editor.

Mr Clarke arranged trips to Paris and Switzerland for the third and fourth years.

Chris Cooper

We were the first class in the school's history to have French lessons, from Mr Dadds. This led, in the second year, to a very memorable week's trip to Paris. We stayed in what seemed to be luxurious accommodation at the Foyer des Lyceennes. We were mostly in single rooms, with bidets in the bathrooms bearing a notice "This is not a footbath".

Glyn Tucker

We left school in 1955 and quite a few of us went on to the Colleges but in the summer of that year Mr Wicks and Miss Newman were taking a group of pupils to Switzerland and several of us were able to go back and go as senior helpers,

Anthea Croucher

Relaxing in Switzerland

In 1956 I went on the school holiday to Switzerland. To the best of my memory there was about a dozen of us. The teachers were Miss Newman and Mr Wicks. I think we went for a week. During our time there we went by train up the Jungfrau to 13333 feet. We also went to Berne and a few other tourist attractions. We went to Interlaken to a show in the Kursaal and for walks over the hills outside Wilderswil.

Shirley Tanton slipped over on a rock and broke her leg and when we got back to Folkestone customs wanted to take the plaster off but were persuaded not to. I have in my hand the Identity Card we were issued with for the trip. It is dated 23 June 1956 and signed by Mr Cook.

Rodney Betts

1960s

The school returned to Switzerland regularly over the next ten years. This photograph was taken in the 1960s.

A trip to the Houses of Parliament in 1960

1970s

School trips I remember are :

Dungeness Power Station and Camber Sands.
A walking weekend Youth Hostling with Miss Le-Page.
Wimbledon quarterfinals.
An athletics trip to Crystal Palace - I should have been running 800 metres but I chickened out!

Sharon Crowley

1980s

Water sports in France during the 1980s

2000s

This History department organises an annual trip to Belgium to visit the war graves, and the PE Department takes a group to Andorra to ski each year.

Fundraising

1950s

The Bulldog magazine of 1952 mentions the 'huge parcel of clothing for the refugees', possibly for flood victims in Devon.

Editor

1960s

The school magazine reported on a 'Rave Up in the Canteen' in 1968, at which a student pop group called 'Nameless' raised £4 towards the School Fund.

1970s

The School Walk was started in 1975, when the whole school walked to Sandown Castle in Deal and back, raising money for charity by sponsorship. The walk continues to this day. The first walk raised £2,000 towards a new minibus.

The Oxfam Blanket Drive of 1973 was a huge success, and 60 blankets were made or collected.

I can remember a Summer Fete on the school field. I think it was only for the pupils, but not sure. Mr Rosseter's coconut ice was always a hit

Sharon Crowley

My form got landed annually with the sale of cocoa-nut ice. It made a lot of money for the school funds, but I do not wish ever to see a piece of that sweetmeat again!

Mr Rosseter, writing in 1985

1980s

During my time at school a lot of fund raising took place for the Sports Centre, which opened the year I left and for local charities including the Martha House Trust. Residents of Martha House would sometime be the special guests at our Friday assembly.

Stella Leitner

2000s

The school works with The Samaritans to send shoeboxes full of gifts to underprivileged children each Christmas and has a varied programme of fundraising events, including the annual school walk, now in its 34th year.
Editor

The School Production

1950s

The school plays were put on in the quad when I was at the school. I remember the play in 1953 was *'The Merchant of Venice'*.

Rodney Betts

The cast of the Merchant of Venice

The play that I took part in at Sandwich School was Sheridan's *"The Rivals"*. I played the part of Fag, the manservant. Not a major role but it was a fun evening

Ron Brown

'The Rivals'

The nativity play was one of the features of the year. I was given the role of Joseph. It took place in what was then the hall and gym, on the opposite side of the quad to the new hall.

Glyn Tucker

The Nativity Play from 1954

Mr. Wicks. He was a scary chap! Head of Wingham House. They won everything - they were afraid not to! He produced the school plays, and did the off stage screams. No one else would put enough drama into them, he said.

Andrew Frost

1960s

School play 1960

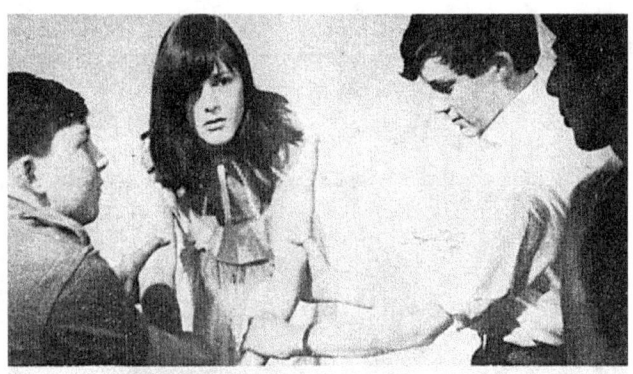

A scene from "Antigone"—last year's schoolplay.

A scene from Antigone (1967)

1970s

We also had a pantomime that first year called *'Babes in the Wood'* written and produced by Mrs. O'Niel the drama teacher and Mr. Probert the rural studies teacher (he was a fantastic Baron Moneybags!). I can remember the thrilling excitement of actually being in a performance on stage and although I played a part as a villager and, therefore, didn't have a speaking part I fell over on the first night with Mrs. O'Niel and we just carried on acting so everyone thought it was part of the performance. Absolutely brilliant! Loved every single minute of it and it was hard work but tremendous fun.

Linda Ridden

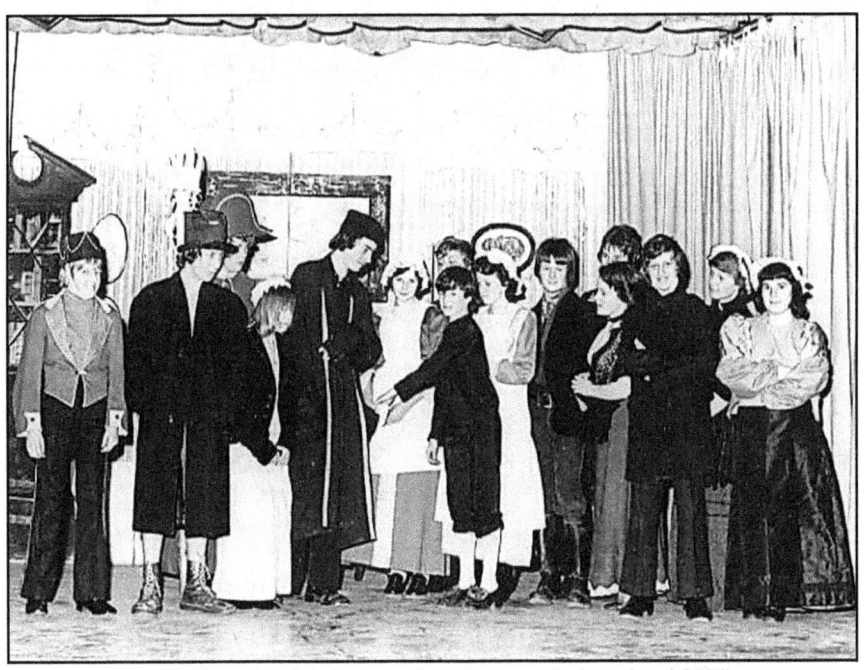

'*Oliver!*' which ran for three nights in 1977.

1980s

School productions led by Mr Matthews and Mr Shaw included '*Bugsy Malone*', '*Cinderelli*' (a spin off of Cinderella including ice-cream) and '*Joseph with his Amazing Technicolor Dream Coat*'.

Stella Leitner

Mother Courage from 1983

1990s

In 1995, the play Odysseus, written by Mr Shaw, with music by Mrs Maxfield was performed in London's Queen Elizabeth Halls as part of the Barclays Music Theatre Awards. The performance won three awards.

2000s

Quince and Bottom in the school performance of *A Midsummer Night's Dream*, which played at The Gulbenkian Theatre in Canterbury and in Singapore during 2002.

The school returned to The Gulbenkian again in 2010 with a production of *Les Miserables.*

Appendix 1
List of Pupils on Roll September 1935

Those in bold are siblings (asterisks denote twins). My apologies for any errors, which are a result of my misreading the 1935 manuscript text.

Surname	First Name	Born	Home village
Adams	Dorothy	1921	Woodnesborough
Agley	Leonard	1922	Eastry
Ainsworth	Leonard	1921	Sandwich
Alexander	Olive	1923	Worth
Allen	Kenneth	1922	Sandwich
Amos	John	1922	Sandwich
Andrews	**Jean**	1923	Tilmanstone
Andrews	**Harold**	1924	Tilmanstone
Arnold	Kenneth	1923	Sandwich
Ashington	Grace	1923	Eastry
Ashman	Margaret	1921	Woodnesborough
Ashman	James	1923	Woodnesborough
Atkins	**Mark**	1921	Eastry
Atkins	**Cyril**	1923	Eastry
Avery	Joyce	1921	Deal
Bailey	**Horace**	1922	Betteshanger
Bailey	**Gladys**	1923	Betteshanger
Bailey	Ivy	1923	Sandwich
Ball	Benjamin	1921	Betteshanger
Ballard	George	1923	Sandwich
Barham	Cecil	1923	Eastry
Barn	Jessie	1922	Sandwich
Barnstead	Paul	1922	Betteshanger
Bartlett	Harold	1922	Woodnesborough
Batchelor	**Fred**	1922	Sandwich
Batchelor	**Joyce**	1923	Sandwich
Batchelor	Ella	1923	Sandwich
Bates	**Colin**	1921	Eastry
Bates	**Elizabeth**	1923	Eastry

Bax	**Jean**	1922	Sandwich
Bax	**Constance**	1923	Sandwich
Bax	Eva	1923	Eastry
Bax	Reginald	1923	Sandwich
Bean	Douglas	1922	Sandwich
Beck	Freda	1921	Sandwich
Bedwell	**Vera**	1921	Richborough
Bedwell	**Alfred**	1923	Richborough
Beer	Margaret	1922	Eastry
Beer	Ronald	1923	Sandwich
Bennett	George	1922	Eastry
Bennett	Dorothy	1922	Sandwich
Betts	Robert	1921	Woodnesborough
Betts	Edward	1923	Eastry
Bird	Robert	1921	Sandwich
Boughton	Gladys	1922	Eastry
Bourner	Marjorie	1921	Sandwich
Boyd	Dennis	1922	Sandwich
Boyd	Francis	1924	Sandwich
Bramble	Cyril	1922	Eastry
Bramble	Pearl	1923	Sholden Bank
Brett	**Cyril**	1921	Sandwich
Brett	**Norah**	1922	Sandwich
Brett	Frank	1922	Sandwich
Brett	Joyce	1923	Sandwich
Brett	**Arthur**	1924	Sandwich
Bright	Margaret	1923	Eastry
Brooker	**Eileen**	1921	Eastry
Brooker	**Thomas**	1923	Eastry
Bugg	**William**	1921	Eastry
Bugg	**Reginald**	1923	Eastry
Bullock	Raymond	1923	Eastry
Burch	Cyril	1922	Woodnesborough
Burley	Diana	1922	Sandwich
Burr	Betty	1923	Richborough
Burton	Lily	1921	Sandwich
Burton	Doreen	1922	Eastry
Burton	Thomas	1923	Sandwich

Butt	Eileen	1923	Sholden
Capp	Heather	1922	Worth
Capp	Joan	1922	Sandwich
Carr	Josephine	1923	Sholden Bank
Carter	George	1922	Eastry
Carter	Samuel	1922	Eastry
Carty	**Noah**	1921	Sandwich
Carty	**Phyllis**	1923	Sandwich
Castle	Edwin	1923	Sandwich
Champs	Ernest	1922	Sandwich
Cheeseman	**Thomas**	1921	Eastry
Cheeseman	**J Albert**	1924	Eastry
Church	Leonard	1923	Eastry
Claringbould	Leonard	1922	Sandwich
Collard	Robert	1921	Woodnesborough
Coller	Edna	1922	Sholden Bank
Cook	**Joan**	1922	Eastry
Cook	**Edith**	1924	Eastry
Couchman	Annie	1923	Sandwich
Couchman	Maurice	1924	Eastry
Coulson	Lilian	1922	Betteshanger
Court	Stanley	1922	Sholden Bank
Cox	**Florence**	1921	Sandwich
Cox	**Albert**	1923	Sandwich
Cox	Rose	1923	Eastry
Crampton	**Patricia**	1921	Sandwich
Crampton	**Alfred**	1923	Sandwich
Cronk	Edna	1922	Sandwich
Crouch	**Annie**	1921	Sandwich
Crouch	**Arthur**	1922	Sandwich
Cudworth	Kathleen	1922	Sandwich
Cuffley	Fred	1922	Deal
Cuffley	Marjorie	1922	Walmer
Cummings	Edwin	1924	Sandwich
Dale	Frederick	1922	Woodnesborough
Daniels	Evelyn	1921	Woodnesborough
Daniels	Arthur	1923	East Studdall
Davies	**Kenneth**	1923	Betteshanger

Davies	**John**	1924	Betteshanger
Davis	John	1921	Worth
Denham	Henry	1921	Eastry
Denne	Heather	1920	Sandwich
Deveson	Mary	1921	Sandwich
Deveson	Stanley	1922	Eastry
Deveson	Leslie	1924	Eastry
Deveson	Frederick	1924	Eastry
Dewell	Raymond	1923	Woodnesborough
Dibble	John Scott	1924	Sandwich
Dick	David	1923	Betteshanger
Divall	Eric	1923	Little Mongeham
Dogan	Denis	1922	Tilmanstone
Doherty	Robert	1922	Betteshanger
Drayson	Leslie	1923	Sandwich
Driver	William	1923	Eastry
Dunn	Vera	1921	Betteshanger
Dunn	Margaret	1922	Eastry
Eddy	June	1923	Betteshanger
Elbrow	**Ernest**	1921	Worth
Elbrow	**George**	1923	Worth
Eldridge	Joyce	1921	Eastry
Eldridge	**Frederick**	1922	**Finglesham**
Ellender	Edith	1921	Sandwich
Ellender	Nellie	1923	Marshborough
Ellis	Evelyn	1922	Northbourne
Elvery	**Ernest**	1922	Hacklinge
Elvery	**Robert**	1923	Eastry
Evans	**Phyllis**	1921	Northbourne
Evans	**Gwyneth**	1923	Northbourne
Evans	Lavona	1923	Sandwich
Fackenstein	Albert	1922	Stonar
Fagg	Raymond	1922	Sandwich
Fagg	Denis	1923	Tilmanstone
Fagg	Kathleen	1924	Northbourne
Farmer	Phyllis	1922	Sandwich
Fenney	Norman	1921	Northbourne
Field	Gladys	1921	Sandwich

Finnis	Victor	1921	Hacklinge
Fitall	Edith	1921	Finglesham
Folwell	**Connie**	1921	Eastry
Folwell	**Alfred**	1923	Eastry
Fowler	Bryan	1922	Deal
Franks	Elsie	1922	Sandwich
Freeman	**Edward**	1921	Sandwich
Freeman	**Walter**	1923	Sandwich
Friend	Robert	1921	Eastry
Gardner	Fred	1922	Woodnesborough
Garlinge	Blanche	1921	Eastry
Garner	Mary	1923	Betteshanger
Gatehouse	Gladys	1924	Betteshanger
Gibb	Thomas	1922	Betteshanger
Gibbons	John	1923	Eastry
Gibbons	Joan	1923	Ash
Gibson	Robert	1924	Eastry
Giles	Mabel	1921	Eastry
Giles	**Leonard**	1922	Betteshanger
Giles	**Kenneth**	1923	Betteshanger
Gills	Mary	1923	Eastry
Godden	Kathleen	1921	Northbourne
Goodbar	Herbert	1922	Ham
Gooodson	Reginald	1922	Eastry
Goswell	Lydia	1922	Eastry
Gower	Kathleen	1922	Finglesham
Grant	**Sidney**	1921	Betteshanger
Grant	**William**	1923	Betteshanger
Griffiths	Leslie	1923	Sandwich
Groombridge	Gladys	1921	Sandwich
Guthrie *	**Margaret**	1921	Betteshanger
Guthrie *	**Ian**	1921	Betteshanger
Hampson	**Violet**	1921	Sandwich
Hampson	**Kathleen**	1923	Sandwich
Hanes	Gilbert	1922	Studdal
Hare	Rosina	1923	Northbourne
Harffey	Clement	1922	Eastry
Harle *	**Eustace**	1921	Sandwich

Harle *	**Raymond**	1921	Sandwich
Harper	Ronald	1923	Eastry
Harris	Margaret	1923	Eastry
Harrop	Sidney	1921	Woodnesborough
Harvey	George	1923	Finglesham
Hayward	Arthur	1921	Betteshanger
Hayward	Charles	1923	Sandwich
Hearn	Margaret	1922	Sandwich
Hedgecock	Richard	1922	Sandwich
Hellis	Jean	1921	Upper Deal
Hewitt	Winnie	1921	Little Mongeham
Hibberd	William	1922	Sholden Bank
Hickmore	George	1921	Sandwich
Hickton	Jean	1924	Eastry
Higgins	John	1921	Sandwich
Hills	Frederick	1922	Eastry
Hirst	Arthur	1923	Betteshanger
Histed	Audrey	1924	Sandwich
Hoile	Fred	1921	Eastry
Hoile	Joan	1923	Sandwich
Holman	Herbert	1923	Sandwich
Holness	Alfred	1922	Worth
Hopper	Mollie	1923	Eastry
Hopper	Monica	1923	Sandwich
Hopper	Glenison	1924	Sandwich
House	Fred	1923	Sholden Bank
Howard	Sylvia	1921	Sandwich
Howard	Millicent	1922	Sandwich
Howard	Frank	1923	Sandwich
Howard	Vera	1923	Sandwich
Howland	Bernard	1921	Worth
Humphrey	Herbert	1922	Eastry
Humphreys	Mary	1922	Finglesham
Hurst	Norah	1921	Sandwich
Hutchings	Maud	1924	Betteshanger
Jackson	Freda	1922	Studdall
James	Sylvia	1922	Northbourne
Jeffery	Alice	1923	Eastry

Jones	Eileen	1921	Sandwich
Kemp	Jeffrey	1922	Eastry
Kemp	Alice	1922	Eastry
Kemp	Sidney	1922	Sandwich
Kemp	**Frank**	1922	Sandwich
Kemp	**Alan**	1923	Sandwich
Kemp	Lydia	1923	Eastry
Kemp	George	1923	Eastry
Kemp	Danny	1923	Eastry
Kimber	Margaret	1922	Sandwich
Kimber	Hilda	1924	Sandwich
King	Sidney	1921	Eastry
Kirby	Gladys	1922	Northourne
Kirby	Leonard	1923	Deal
Kirk	**Gladys**	1923	Betteshanger
Kirk	**Doreen**	1924	Betteshanger
Knight	Phyllis	1923	Woodnesborough
Knight	Alex	1923	Sandwich
Knowler	Phyllis	1922	Sholden
Ladd	Lawrence	1921	Eastry
Ladd	**Eric**	1921	Eastry
Ladd	**Lillian**	1923	Eastry
Laker	Edward	1923	Eastry
Langley	Daphne	1921	Sandwich
Langridge *	**Alfred**	1923	Sholden
Langridge *	**Richard**	1923	Sholden
Lapish	Stuart	1921	Sandwich
Larkins	Winifred	1921	Hacklinge
Larkins	**Dennis**	1923	Eastry
Larkins	**Rita**	1924	Eastry
Law	Harold	1922	Sandwich
Lawrence	Victor	1922	Little Mongeham
Lees	Mark	1921	East Studdal
Leith	Joan	1923	Sandwich
Lelliot	**Ivy**	1924	Eastry
Lelliott	**George**	1921	Eastry
Long	Reginald	1923	Worth
Lumbard	Joyce	1923	Sandwich

Mallet	Edward	1923	Mongeham
Marley	Frances	1924	Eastry
Marsh	Maud	1922	Sandwich
Marsh	John	1923	Sandwich
Marsh	Louise	1923	Sandwich
Marshall	**Ruby**	**1921**	**Hacklinge**
Marshall	**Thomas**	**1923**	**Sholden**
Martin	Kenneth	1922	Sandwich
Martin	Ronald	1922	Eastry
Maxted	Rose	1921	Eastry
Maxwell	Noreen	1921	Sholden
May	Frank	1923	Sandwich
Maybury	Maureen	1922	Ash
Mills	Edgar	1923	Worth
Mills	Gilbert	1921	Eastry
Minter	Evelyn	1921	L. Statenborough
Moat	Jack	1922	Deal
Morris	Sylvia	1921	Sandwich
Morris	Joyce	1921	Sandwich
Morris	**Stanley**	**1921**	**Sandwich**
Morris	**Eunice**	**1924**	**Sandwich**
Mottershead	Herbert	1922	Sholden
Munk	**Bernice**	**1920**	**Betteshanger**
Munk	**Joan**	**1923**	**Betteshanger**
Nadin	Kathleen	1922	Northbourne
Newham	Leslie	1922	Eastry
Newmark	Violet	1921	Sandwich
Northrop	Roy	1921	Finglesham
Nower	Winifred	1921	Sandwich
Nutley	Joan	1923	Sandwich
Oliver	James	1922	Sholden
Overton	Christabel	1923	Sandwich
Owen	John	1923	Sandwich
Page	Edna	1920	Ash
Page	Elsie	1922	Sandwich
Page	Thomas	1922	Eastry
Page	Edward	1923	Sandwich
Pain	Minnie	1922	Eastry

Parfitt	**Wilfred**	1921	Sutton
Parfitt	**Harold**	1922	Sutton
Parfitt	Joseph	1922	Studdal
Parker	June	1924	Sandwich
Parmenter *	**Harry**	1922	Sutton
Parmenter *	**John**	1922	Sutton
Pashley	Enid	1924	Each End
Paterson	William	1922	Betteshanger
Pemble	Olive	1923	Hacklinge
Penn	Eileen	1921	Eastry
Percival	Margaret	1921	Woodnesborough
Perkins	Dennis	1921	Sandwich
Petley	June	1924	Sandwich
Pettican	Frank	1922	Sandwich
Philpott	Edward	1921	Woodnesborough
Phipps	Dennis	1923	Eastry
Pilcher	Reginald	1922	Woodnesborough
Pilcher	William	1922	Northbourne
Pilcher	**Charles**	1922	Betteshanger
Pilcher	**Edith**	1923	Betteshanger
Pilcher	Irene	1923	Betteshanger
Pittock	Elsie	1922	Sandwich
Playford	Charles	1922	Eastry
Pointer	Gordon	1922	Eastry
Potter	John	1921	Sandwich
Potts	Dinah	1922	Sandwich
Potts	Olive	1922	Sandwich
Price	**Molly**	1921	Sandwich
Price	John	1922	Northbourne
Price	**Daphne**	1923	Sandwich
Printer	Frederick	1923	Eastry
Prior	Joan	1922	Eastry
Prodgers	Hazel	1921	Sholden Bank
Ratcliff	George	1923	Eastry
Rayment	Peter	1922	Eastry
Read	Ruby	1921	Woodnesborough
Redman	John	1922	Sandwich
Revell	Leslie	1921	Northbourne

Richards	Betty	1923	Betteshanger
Roberts	James	1921	Sandwich
Rose	William	1922	Eastry
Rowley	Ronald	1922	Sandwich
Rowson	William	1922	Betteshanger
Rye	William	1922	Sandwich
Sage	Vera	1924	Sandwich
Saint	**Gwendolyn**	1922	Betteshanger
Saint	**Kathleen**	1923	Betteshanger
Salter	Eunice	1921	Sandwich
Salter	June	1924	Sandwich
Sandwell	**Leslie**	**1921**	**Worth**
Sandwell	**Edna**	**1923**	**Worth**
Saunders	Phyllis	1921	Sholden
Scarborough	George	1923	Eastry
Silk	Patricia	1921	Sandwich
Simm	James	1923	Betteshanger
Simmons	Denis	1921	Sandwich
Sly	Stanley	1923	Eastry
Smallman	Victor	1922	Woodnesborough
Smith	Leonard	1923	Sandwich
Smith	Joyce	1921	Woodnesborough
Smith	Ruby	1921	Sholden
Smith	Henry	1922	Deal
Smith	Rose	1922	Sandwich
Smith	Stuart	1923	Woodnesborough
Snashall	Gladys	1923	Betteshanger
Spain	Frederick	1921	Eastry
Spain	Muriel	1922	Worth
Spain	Nellie	1923	Sandwich
Spencer	George	1923	Betteshanger
Spicer	Joyce	1923	Sandwich
Stanley	Peggy	1922	Sandwich
Steele	Eileen	1923	Eastry
Stevens	Grace	1921	Worth
Stevens	Charles	1922	Worth
Stewart	John	1922	Eastry
Stockley	Edith	1921	Sandwich

Streatfield	Faith	1922	Sandwich
Tandy	Joan	1922	Sandwich
Taylor	Edith	1921	Betteshanger
Taylor	Mary	1922	Sholden
Taylor	Elsie	1923	Eastry
Thomas	Hazel	1923	Sandwich
Thompson	**Olive**	1921	Finglesham
Thompson	**Joseph**	1923	Finglesham
Thompson	Herbert	1923	Sandwich
Thornby	Arthur J	1923	Eastry
Tonkin	Barbara	1921	Sandwich
Townley	Alice	1922	Sholden
Townley	Nelson	1923	Sholden
Townshend	Phyllis	1922	Sandwich
Tritton	Elizabeth	1923	East Studdal
Tuckers	James	1921	East Studdall
Turrell	Leonard	1922	Eastry
Vousden	Sidney	1922	Eastry
Vousden	Yvonne	1923	Eastry
Wager	William	1922	Northbourne
Wager	Raymond	1922	Betteshanger
Wall	Joan	1922	Sandwich
Wallis	Queenie	1923	Eastry
Walls	**Herbert**	1923	Worth
Walls	**Joyce**	1924	Worth
Walter	Doris	1921	Worth
Walton	Lawrence	1921	Betteshanger
Wanstall	Ivy	1921	Sandwich
Warr	George	1921	Eastry
Waters	Doris	1922	Woodnesborough
Webb	Ernest	1923	Tilmanstone
Wells	**Sidney**	1921	Sandwich
Wells	**Henry**	1922	Sandwich
Wells	Margaret	1922	Betteshanger
Westover	Arthur	1923	Northbourne
Whiddett	Edwin	1923	Sandwich
White	Frank	1922	Sandwich
Whittaker	John	1922	Eastry

Wickham	Daphne	1922	Sholden
Wilburn	Douglas	1922	Woodnesborough
Wild	Geoffrey	1923	Betteshanger
Williams	Harold	1922	Eastry
Williams	Edwin	1922	Eastry
Wilmshurst	Lionel	1921	Eastry
Wilson	Florence	1921	Eastry
Wisdom	Alan	1922	Sandwich
Woodcock	Gladys	1921	Eastry
Worth	Alic	1923	Sandwich
York	Benjamin	1922	Sholden
Young	May	1921	Sandwich
Young	Hilda	1922	Hacklinge

www.ingramcontent.com/pod-product-compliance
Lightning Source LLC
LaVergne TN
LVHW022111080426
835511LV00007B/756